ALL PORTUGAL

Photographs: Xavier Durán, Mario Sarria and
FISA-ESCUDO DE ORO photo archive.

Diagrams and reproduction conceived and carried
out in their entirety by the technical teams of
EDITORIAL FISA ESCUDO DE ORO, S.A.

ESCUDO DE ORO

ROMAN TEMPLE AT ÉVORA.

Cradle of many of the greatest discoverers in history, Portugal overlooks the Atlantic Ocean to west and south, gazing out towards the horizon from an immense balcony some 560 kilometres in length, whilst to the east and north it borders with Spain, linked to it not only by geography but also by historic and cultural ties. In essence, the heart of this most westerly of European nations is devoted to the sea, and at every beat of the national heart we can hear the faint echoes of the epic voyages which led so many brave Portuguese sailors to the conquest of new worlds. It was, perhaps, during this period of seafaring exploits that the term *saudade* was first coined. This word perfectly sums up that typically Portuguese mood said to result from a mixture of nostalgia, sadness and melancholy. A way in which this feeling of *saudade* finds expression is in the *fado*, Portugal's most genuine form of popular song, though it has always been more associated with Lisbon and Coimbra than the rest of the country. The words of *fados*, which are like mirrors of the soul, are mostly concerned with feelings such as pain, desperation or sadness, but also happiness and good cheer. Although some historians place the birth of this peculiar branch of popular song as far back as the Middle Ages, it was not until the 19th century that this unusual form of lyrical expression began to achieve fame in the Lisbon districts of Alfama and Bairro Alto. Dressed in dark colours, *fadistas* are usually accompanied by a guitar and a viola, spelling out the rhythmic notes of a musical form as captivating as it is moving.

Including the Azores and Madeira archipelagos, Portugal has a total area of 91,700 square kilometres. The mainland is divided by the River Tagus into two zones which are very different geographically one from another. To the north, the landscape is more undulating, with a succession of plateaux separated by green valleys sloping down gently to the ocean. The region around the banks of the River Douro is much more abrupt, and it is here that we find Malhao da Estrela, whose 1,991 metre peak makes it the highest mountain in continental Portugal. It is surpassed in height only by the volcano Mount Pico, in the Azores, at 2,345 metres. South of the Tagus, the horizon is dominated by vast plains. Only the mountains of the Serra de São Mamede, famed for its caves, dare break the monotony of the landscape.

Radically different from the rest of the country are the physical characteristics of the Azores and Madeira. The two archipelagos, volcanic in origin, contain natural spaces of outstanding beauty and interest. The islands are ringed by high rocky cliffs, the most impressive of them the area around Cape Girão in the south of the island of Madeira, at 560 metres amongst the highest cliffs in the world. Portugal is home to both the Mediterranean and the Atlantic climates, a circumstance which explains the moderate temperatures in winter as well as in summer. Only certain inland regions escape from the warm, damp air coming in from the nearby ocean.

The first human settlements in what we now know as Portugal go back

THE RIVER DOURO FLOWS THROUGH ONE OF THE WILDEST REGIONS OF PORTUGAL.

D. Luís bridge in Porto.

to the late-Neolithic period. This was the time of the first *castros*, small fortified villages of circular huts made from stone and straw. The arrival of the Greeks, Phoenicians and Carthaginians led to the disappearance of these settlements from the central and southern regions of the country, their presence becoming limited to areas north of the River Tagus. Their inhabitants lived near the mountains, dedicated to pasturing. We can now speak of the appearance of the Lusitanians, a people with a very marked personality which put up fierce, heroic resistance to the advance of the Roman legions.

Once the Lusitanians had been finally subjected in the early-2nd century BC, the ensuing Romanisation affected these territories to varying degrees: whilst Roman influence was stronger on the plateau, it was scarcely noted in the mountains of the north.

The identity of what was to become the Portuguese nation began to take shape in the 3rd century with the creation of an autonomous region known as *Gallaecia*. Independent of *Lusitania* and *Tarraconense* provinces, Gallaecia occupied a huge expanse of land around the city of Braga. Over the course of the 5th

and 6th centuries, Braga was one of the capitals of the Suevians, a Germanic people who occupied the country after the fall of the Roman Empire. Some Suevian monarchs also installed their reigns in Guimarães and Portucale, now known as Porto and from whose name that of Portugal is derived.

The Visigoths took over from the Suevians in the year 585 though, reigning from Toledo, they scarcely left their mark on the local population. In 711, the Moors defeated Dom Rodrigo, the last Goth king, and brought the entire Iberian Peninsula under their sway. As had occurred centuries before with the Romans, the north of Portugal was the most impermeable part of the country to the influence of the new conquerors. The Moors settled, basically, in the southern part of the country, giving it the name of *Al Gharb* (Algarve). Whilst all this was taking place, the duchy of Portucale was beginning to rise up in the lands between the rivers Miño and Duero. After the commencement of the Reconquest, Portucale, accorded the status of country as early as the 11th century, was ruled by governors named by the kings of León.

A period then opened in which the dismembering of the Caliphate of Cordoba only facilitated the Catholic Monarchs' objective of expelling the Moors from the Peninsula. At the same time, the Portuguese people's desire for independence grew until Afonso Henriques, grandson of Alfonso VI of Castile and León, self-proclaimed himself the first king of the country in 1143. Alfonso VII finally accepted this state of affairs under the terms of the Treaty of Zamora.

The heirs to this first Portuguese monarch continued to wage war against the Moors until the last of them fled Faro, the last important redoubt still in their power, in 1249. The frontiers of the new kingdom were finally established some years later under the reign of Dom Dinis. On the death of Ferdinand I in 1383, his wife Leonor gave up the throne to her daughter Beatriz, wife of Juan I of Castile. This was a decision which did not meet with the approval of those who feared for the independence of the country. In the ensuring struggle, the supporters of João, Maestre de Avis and brother of the deceased Ferdinand I, defeated the Castilian troops at the Battle of

THE ARCHIPELAGO OF MADEIRA IS A PLACE OF AWE-INSPIRING VIEWS.

THE VILLAGE OF SÃO JORGE, ON THE ISLAND OF MADEIRA.

Aljubarrota in 1385. Thus began the reign of João I, the first member of a dynasty, that of Avis, which was to turn Portugal into a veritable world power.

This was a period in Portuguese history indelibly marked by the figure of Prince Dom Enrique the Navigator, who backed many maritime expeditions culminating in the discovery of the islands of Madeira (1419) and the Azores (1427), and the exploration of much of West Africa. This enterprise was continued in the following years under the reigns of Afonso V and João II. In 1447, Vasco de Gama opened up a new trade route to India, and in 1500, Pedro Álvarez Cabral reached the coasts of Brazil.

Nevertheless, Portugal enjoyed its period of maximum splendour and prosperity with the arrival on the throne of Manuel I (1495-1521). Portuguese control of the world's main trading ports soon led to greater income to the state treasury. Manueline architecture arose as a form of artistic expression reflecting not only the economic boom but also the extension of the limits of the Portuguese empire. Nevertheless, having attained this zenith, the country fell into a financial and dynastic crisis which ended in 1580 with the proclamation of Philip II of Spain as king of Portugal under the name of Philip I. Spanish domination lasted 60 years, until the Duke of Bragança was crowned as Portugal's new king under the name of João IV. Spain, however, did not recognise the sovereignty of the neighbouring nation until 1668. Seven years previously, Portugal and England had signed a co-operation agreement

STATUE OF THE MARQUIS OF POMBAL, AN EMINENT FIGURE IN PORTUGUESE HISTORY.

MONUMENT TO THE DISCOVERIES IN LISBON.

which lasted practically until the 20th century.

The 18th century saw the application of the principles of enlightened despotism in Portugal. A secretary of state, the Marquis of Pombal, was the principal instigator of this regime. An economic policy based on liberalised made a decisive contribution to the reformation and modernisation of the country's outmoded structures. Amongst other things, the layout city of Lisbon, which had been almost completely destroyed by an earthquake in 1755, was redesigned. As in Spain, the 19th century was marked by continuous disputes between the most absolutist sectors of society and the supporters of the liberal ideas which were beginning to take hold all over Europe. The prolonged situation of instability finally affected the credibility of the monarchy, which was abolished in 1910

and the Republic proclaimed. The first republican governments were scarcely more fortunate than the monarchy, however, and in 1926 the army rose up and took power. Six years later, António Oliveira Salazar was installed to power. During Salazar's mandate, the so-called *Estado Novo* (New State) was installed. This was a system based on a political model which, though it gave Portugal a modern economy, caused serious damage to broad sectors of society and strictly limited civil liberties. In 1968, Salazar

left the presidency of the nation in the hands of Marcelo Caetano, who began a timid, insufficient process of political aperture. Finally, on 25 April 1974, a bloodless military coup which has become known historically as the Revolution of the Carnations, put an end to almost 70 years of dictatorship and laid the foundations of modern-day Portugal.

Portugal is now a fully-consolidated democracy which has joined its destiny to that of its fellow members of the European Union, of which it has been a member since 1986.

PENEDA-GERÊS NATIONAL PARK.

Portugal's largest nature reserve, the only one in the country with the category of National Park, occupies an area of some 70,000 hectares straddling Minho and Trás-os-Montes provinces at the southernmost point in Portuguese territory. Generous rainfall and the benign local climate, a mixture of the Atlantic and Mediterranean climates, here produces the most diverse and abundant vegetation. As the altitude increases, we see from olives, vines and orange trees to pine and oak woods. The peaks of these mountains are formed by defiant granite outcrops. Besides it flora and fauna, the Peneda-Gerês National Park is also reach in archaeological sites testifying to the presence of human settlement here since time immemorial.

OVERALL VIEW OF THE PARK AND ONE OF ITS ENTRANCES.

VIANA DO CASTELO: PRAÇA DA REPÚBLICA.

An important sea port during the period of the discoveries, Viana do Castelo is a monumental city which lies at the mouth of the River Lima. The presence here of numerous noble old houses speak to us of a glorious past whose star began to fade with the loss of Brazil as a colony. The city centre is formed by the splendid **Praça da República**, presided over by a Renaissance fountain and framed by fine 16th-century buildings. Some of the most emblematic of these are the palaces known as the **Palácios do Conselho**, whose solid bearing makes them a faithful reflection of the Gothic style of the period, the **Hospital of A Misericórdia** and the church of the same name. Near the square rises the silhouette of the **Cathedral,** or **Sé**. Also built in the Gothic style, the cathedral contains a fine work representing the Baptism of Christ.

In secluded little **Praça de Erva**, an example of the Manueline style, stands the former hospital which attended to the needs of pilgrims on their way to Santiago.

Another of Viana do Castelo's most important attractions is the **City Museum** (Museu Municipal), housed in an old palace. Besides testimony to the past wealth of the city, the museum also contains rooms devoted to the local folklore and to Portuguese ceramics and painting.

One of the finest viewpoints from which to calmly observe the entire city and the mouth of the River Lima is the **Basilica of Santa Luzia**, which stands on the mount of the same name. This neo-Byzantine work dates from 1903 and is reached by a funicular railway line which has its point of origin at the railway station. The hill also contains the remains of an ancient pre-Roman fortress.

According to legend, a pilgrim on his way to Santiago de Compostela was condemned to death by hanging at his pass through Barcelos, having been unjustly accused of stealing some object of value. Shortly before the sentence was carried out, the condemned man commended his soul to Saint James. In answer to his prayers, the roast chickens the judge in charge of the case was about to eat started to sing. This is the origin of the famed Barcelos cockerel, universal symbol of Portugal and one of the reasons behind the international reputation of the local ceramics.

But besides these, the craftsmen of Barcelos also make other types of product (ceramics, wickerwork, embroidery, etc) which may be less famous but are, nonetheless, of the highest quality.

Some of the most important sites to visit in this city are the **Regional Ceramics Museum**, the **Matriz Church** and the **Church of O Senhor Jesus da Cruz**, adorned with artistic glazed tiles.

CROSS OF THE LEGEND OF THE COCKEREL.

GLAZED TILES IN THE MATRIZ CHURCH.

BRAGA: PRAÇA DA REPÚBLICA.

Ancient Roman *Bracara Augusta*, once Suevian and Visigoth capital, is now a city rightfully proud of its past and embellished by a huge artistic heritage which amply demonstrates the powerful role played by the church throughout its long history. It is no surprise, therefore, that one of Braga's principal poles of tourist attraction should be its Easter celebrations, nor that its most outstanding building should be the **Cathedral** or **Sé**.

Rua do Souto, which runs through the historic heart of the city, leads to the Cathedral, built at the command of the count and countess of Portucale, Henry of Burgundy and his wife Teresa. Of the original Romanesque structure, all that remains is the nave ground plan, the Sun Gate on the south side, a frieze running along the external walls and the cloister apse. Successive alterations carried out on the church explain the presence of Gothic elements and the baroque style which dominates the interior. One of the chapels around the cloister, the Chapel of the Monarchs, contains the tombs of Henry of Burgundy and Lady Teresa. The mortal remains of Archbishop Lourenço Vicente, a hero of the Battle of Aljubarrota, also lie here.

Not far away are the **house and chapel of Os Coimbras**, both dating from the early 16th-century, and which are important elements in the city's Manueline heritage.

Outstanding amongst Braga's many monuments are the baroque **Pelican Fountain**, emblazoned with the coat of arms of Archbishop Gaspar de Bragança; the **Benedictine Monastery of Tibaes**, and the **Church of Nossa Senhora do Povo**, built by the same architect responsible for the **Sanctuary of O Bom Jesus do Monte**.

CHURCH OF NOSSA SENHORA DO POVO.

A long granite and plaster stairway along which are nine fountains, leads to this neo-classical sanctuary which looks out over the city from the top of a hill. This spot, the destination of many pilgrimages, is surrounded by the lovely gardens which make up the park also known as that of O Bom Jesus do Monte. Finally, some three kilometres outside Braga are one of the few sites remaining to testify to the Visigoth presence in this area: the tiny **Church of São Frutuoso de Montelios**, in the village of **São Jerónimo Real**.

CHAPEL OF OS COIMBRAS.
SANCTUARY OF O BOM JESUS DO MONTE.

THE CASTLE AND WALLS.

Encircling the old part of the city, double city walls in a perfect state of conservation remind us that Bragança was once a military fortress. Though the origins of its **castle** go back to the late-12th century, Celts, Romans, Visigoths and Moors had already settled on this site in previous historical periods.

The impressive Keep, which now houses the **Bragança Military Museum**, presides an architectural site which also includes the **Domus Municipalis**, the only Romanesque civil building still standing in Portugal.

The interior of the **Cathedral** or **Sé**, with its simple façade, is decorated in an exuberant baroque

DOMUS MUNICIPALIS.

style. Also interesting is the **Abade Baçal Museum**, which offers a complete review of the different civilisations which have occupied the city over its long history.

GUIMARÃES CASTLE, WHERE THE FIRST KING OF PORTUGAL WAS BORN.

A plaque bearing the inscription "Portugal was born here" welcomes all visitors to this historic city where, in effect, Afonso Henriques, first king of Portugal, was born. The happy event took place in Vimaranes Castle, from whose name that of the city is derived. This ancient fortress stands north of the old city centre, an attractive labyrinth of streets and squares of medieval origin whose ancient charm has been wisely conserved. Still standing in the castle are the Keep, seven minor turrets and part of the walls. Along the path which descends towards the centre of Guimarães stands the Romanesque **Hermitage of São Miguel**, which dates from the 12th century. Opposite this beautiful little building rises the imposing silhouette of the **Palace of the Dukes of Bragança**. This ancient feudal residence, a remarkable example of early-15th-century Gothic architecture, was built according to the model of the French castles of the Loire region. The palace contains an interesting collection of tapestries and furniture, whilst the roof of the building sports with evident pride a total of 39 brick chimneys.

Taking Rua de Santa Maria, where the continuous presence of medieval mansions gives one the impression that time has stopped forever in that distant period, we come to the former **Convent of Santa Clara**, now the Town Hall. Various rooms from the nearby **Church of Nossa Senhora da Oliveira**, whose origins go back to the 10th century, moreover, house the interesting Alberto Sampaio Museum. The outstanding elements in this church include the Romanesque cloister, dating from the mid-13th century, the statue of Saint Margaret (15th century) and the church treasure, particularly a chalice and a Gothic reliquary.

Also of interest are the baroque

HERMITAGE OF SÃO MIGUEL.

Church of Os Santos Passos, the **Pousada de Santa Maria de Costa**, an outstanding medieval convent and the park known as the **Parque da Penha**, which lies on a hill commanding lovely views over the city.

Mention apart deserves the **Church of São Francisco**, built in the 15th century and altered in the 17th. The walls of the church are decorated with different scenes from the life of the saint reproduced in glazed tiles, whilst the Renaissance cloister with its central fountain is another outstanding element.

PALACE OF THE DUKES OF BRAGANÇA, A SPLENDID EXAMPLE OF PORTUGUESE GOTHIC.

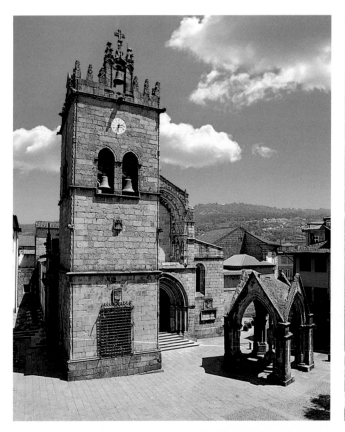

CHURCH OF NOSSA SENHORA DA OLIVEIRA.

CHURCH OF OS SANTOS PASSOS.

LARGO DO TORAL, THE HEART OF THE CITY OF GUIMARÃES.

VIEW OF PORTO.

Situated on the right bank of the River Douro, near the river mouth, the city of Porto disputes with Lisbon the status of economic capital of the country, as well as the honour of being considered the most beautiful city in Portugal, for its old city has been registered on the UNESCO list of World Heritage since 1997. What is beyond discussion is the key role played by Porto in the process of creating the Lusitanian nation. Here, we must remember that Porto was the principal administrative centre of the duchy of Portucale, whose territory extended between the Miño and the Duero, and which finally gave its name renown to what is now Portugal.

The name Porto derives from that of Portucale, which is itself a derivation of the names of two settlements which in ancient times stood on either side of the Duero: Portus and Cale. The duchy of Portucale, for centuries the domain of the monarchs of León, became independent after the marriage of Teresa, daughter of Alfonso VI of León, to Henry of Burgundy. From this union was born Afonso Henriques who, in 1143, was to be proclaimed first king of Portugal. After the final expulsion of the Moors, the centre of gravity shifted to Lisbon and other cities, and Porto was relegated to a second plane.

It was not until the 15th century that Porto rose up once more to play an important role in the history of the country. Many of the ships involved in the great Portuguese voyages of discovery were built in the shipyards of Porto. When Enrique the Navigator decided to undertake the conquest of Ceuta, all the cattle in the region was requisitioned by the local authorities, its owners allowed to keep only the innards or tripe. This led to the creation of the well-known dish "tripas a la porteña", a local speciality, at this time, as well as explaining the nickname of "tripeiros" ("tripers") by which the people of Porto are often known.

During the first half of the 18th century, many British wine merchants became established in Porto. The Treaty of Methwen, signed in 1703, gave them almost complete control

THE ORIGINS OF PORTO CATHEDRAL GO BACK TO THE 12TH CENTURY.

over the wines produced on this side of the Duero. Some years previously, in 1678, the fine wine of Porto had been exported for the first time to a foreign country, in this case to Great Britain.

Famous, then, for its wines, but also for its industry, its enormous cultural heritage and its deeply-rooted traditions, Porto is a constantly developing city and one of the most important economic motors in the entire country.

THE SQUARE IN FRONT OF THE CATHEDRAL.

THE CHURCH OF SÃO FRANCISCO MAIN FACADE.

The most picturesque and ancient districts of this capital of Northern Portugal huddle around the Cathedral and the banks of the river. The **Cathedral** or **Sé** is a remarkable building with the appearance of a fortress and whose origins go back to the Romanesque period, though it has since been altered on various occasions, particularly in the 17th and 18th, when it received its present aspect. The ground plan and the rose window over the entrance date to the late-12th century, whilst the cloister, which contains magnificent glazed tile, is Gothic in style and the portal, the chapels radiating off the nave and two aisles and the high altar are examples of the baroque.

Completing the Cathedral site, the **Episcopal Palace** and the **Church of Os Grilos** are a further two outstanding exponents of the abundant baroque works in the city.

Behind the cathedral, we can make out the Manueline façade of the **Church of Santa Clara**, built in the 15th and 16th centuries though altered years later. The most outstanding element here is the Mudéjar coffering which covers the choir stalls.

Vying in beauty with this church, the **Church of São Francisco** surprises the visitor due to the richness of its internal decoration. As in the Church of Santa Clara, every nook and corner of the building is populated with gilt wood carvings. Goth-

TWO HUNDRED KILOGRAMS OF GOLD POWDER WERE USED TO DECORATE THE INTERIOR OF THE CHURCH OF SÃO FRANCISCO.

THE PALACE OF A BOLSA.

ic in ground plan, the church, which began to be built towards the end of the 14th century, also contains elements of Manueline art, visible in the windows of the south front, and the baroque style, reflected in the ornamental exuberance we find here. Beside it, the **Palace of A Bolsa** is a notable example of the taste for the neo-classic. Of the many apartments in this palace, particularly outstanding are the Golden Room, the Court of the Ancient Trade Tribunal and the Arabic Room, this last a perfect exponent of the oriental airs which

THE STATUE OF PEDRO IV PRESIDES OVER PRAÇA DA LIBERDADE.

THE SÃO BENTO STATION.

impregnate much 19th-century Portuguese architecture.

Further north is **Praça da Liberdade**, the veritable nerve-centre of the city, presided over by the equestrian statue of King Pedro IV. On one side is **São Bento Station**, its main vestibule decorated with white and blue glazed tiles illustrating different moments in the history of Porto.

On the other flank of this square rises the lordly silhouette of the **Tower of the Church of Os Clérigos**, probably the most representative monument in the city. Some 75 metres in height, it was built between 1748 and 1763 in the baroque style. A steep staircase of 225 steps leads up to the highest point in the tower, from which the visitor can enjoy fine views over the entire city. The tower was designed by the Italian architect Nasoni, who also built many more of the churches of Porto. The church front is a fine example of Rococo art.

Another of the city's best-known towers is the **Clocktower**, which rises in the middle of the Town Hall's great front. This building, dating from 1920, communicates with Praça da Liberdade through Avenida dos Aliados.

The **Church of O Carmo**, near that of the Carmelites, dating from the 17th century and a neighbour, also, of the University, is further confir-

TOWER OF OS CLÉRIGOS, VISIBLE FROM MANY POINTS OF PORTO.

THE CHURCH OF O CARMO.

mation to all those who believe Porto to be the Portuguese capital of baroque art. Built in the 18th century, its construction follows the canons of this ornate architectural style, faithfully reflected in the façade with its three sections. The church has a single nave, the outstanding element in the interior being the paintings in the dome over the high altar. On one side of the building stands the graceful Fountain of the Winged Lions, accentuating the beauty of the site even further, if such be possible.

Further away from the city centre, standing on the top of a small hill, the **Church of Santo Ildefonso**, dating from the 18th century, is yet another demonstration of the massive presence of the baroque here, as well as for the abundant use of glazed tiles as a decorative element in fronts and walls. The entrance doorway, flanked by two robust towers, is crowned by a simple triangular pediment. The glazed tiles, dating to 1920, represent different scenes from the life of the saint and allegories of the Eucharist.

But, apart from its monuments, the image of Porto is also closely-linked to its bridges, gigantic marvels of civil engineering which, as well as serving to communicate the two banks, also possess sufficient aesthetic value to make them well worth a visit.

The furthest of these bridges from the sea is **Maria Pia bridge**, crossed endlessly by railway traffic. It was designed by Gustave Eiffel and com-

FRONT OF THE CHURCH OF SANTO ILDEFONSO, WITH ITS GLAZED TILES DEPICTING SCENES FROM THE LIFE OF THE SAINT.

THE LUÍS I BRIDGE.

pleted in 1877. With a metallic structure, the bridge has a single span elevating the railway lines to some 60 metres over the River Douro. Without doubt, however, the most popular of all the bridges of Porto is that of **D. Luís I**, which joins the city centre with the nearby town of Vila Nova de Gaia. It was built in 1886, designed by Teófilo Seyring, a disciple of Eiffel who followed the teachings of his master down to the last detail. Also metallic and with a single span, the viaduct has two storeys

THE TYPICAL BOATS KNOWN AS "RABELOS" STILL PLY THE WATERS OF THE RIVER DOURO.

THE NACIONAL SOARES DOS REIS MUSEUM.

As for Porto's museums, the most interesting is the **Nacional Soares dos Reis Museum**, which contains works by Portuguese sculptor Soares dos Reis as well as those of other Portuguese artists. It is housed in the lovely Palace of Os Carrancas, where the English General Wellington once stayed just a few years before finally defeating Napoleon at the Battle of Waterloo.

Another attraction of Porto is its world-famous wine. The Romans themselves were able to sample the quality of these wines after conquering the Douro region as far back as 48 BC. Although actually produced a few kilometres outside the city, it is in Porto itself that the wineries are to be found. The wine barrels used to be transport across the river by the popular *rabelos*, flat-bottomed boats with two rows of oars and a central sail. Nowadays, more sophisticated means of transport have replaced these traditional vessels which, nonetheless, can still be seen solemnly plying the waters of the Douro.

for vehicle traffic. The upper level has a total length of 392 metres, whilst the second, closer to the river, is 174 metres in length.

The **Arrábida bridge** was completed in 1963, the work of Portuguese engineer Edgar Cardoso, who remained faithful to the tradition of using a single span, though in this case the material employed was concrete. A forth bridge, that of **São João**, for railway transport, dates from 1961, whilst a fifth, the **Freixo bridge** was opened to vehicle traffic in 1996.

THE WINES OF PORTO HAVE GIVEN THIS PICTURESQUE PORTUGUESE CITY WORLDWIDE FAME.

THESE "MOLICEIROS" WERE ONCE USED TO TRANSPORT ALGAE.

The "Portuguese Venice", the "City of Salt" and even the "Miniature Holland", these are just three of the many expressions which popular ingenuity has created to describe Aveiro, without doubt one of the loveliest cities in the whole of Portugal. The explanation for such a wide range of nicknames lies in the city's geographical location. Lying on the banks of a river estuary, water penetrates the city along a network of canals on which sail *moliceiros*, gaily-decorated boats once used to transport algae.

Moreover, the saltworks of Aveiro were known even in the most ancient of days, and many northern European countries still export the salt extracted from them.

But Aveiro also deserves to be called the "City of Glazed Tiles" due to the many buildings whose fronts and interiors feature this decorative element. A good example is the **Church of A Mesicórdia**, built in the 16th century in the baroque style. Opposite is the **Palace of O Conselho**, built in the 18th century.

Another outstanding monument in Aveiro is the Convent of Jesus, now converted into the **Aveiro Museum**. With a Gothic layout and baroque front, the consequence of alterations, this church contains the mortal remains of Saint Joana, patron saint of the city, who spent her final years in the convent. The muse-

THE CHURCH OF A MESICÓRDIA.

um rooms contains important collections of Portuguese art, featuring painting, ceramics and precious metal work.

THE VISEU CATHEDRAL.

Viseu was founded by the Celts and occupied by the Romans in the 2nd century. It stands on a promontory from which it commands fine views of a beautiful landscape of forest and vineyard. The town's most interesting buildings flank a broad square presided over by a Renaissance-style cross. The **cathedral**, dating from the 13th century, contains the habitual combination of different styles due to successive renovation: the two towers on the front and the columns in the interior are Romanesque, whilst the vault arches are Manueline in style and the clois- ter is built in accordance with Renaissance canons. Beside it, the **Grão Vasco Museum** houses works by the painter of the same name, as well as glazed tiles from the 17th century. Also worth a visit is the **Church of A Mesicórdia** with its twin bell- towers and marked baroque style.

17TH-CENTURY GLAZED TILES IN THE GRÃO VASCO MUSEUM.

THE CHURCH OF A MESICÓRDIA.

PRAÇA LUÍS DE CAMÕES.

Thanks to its privileged position at the top of a hill over one thousand metres high, A Guarda played an important role in the Middle Ages in the defence of the territorial integrity of Portugal against the expansionist aspirations of the Crown of Castile. Traces from this period can still be found here in the historic centre of a city whose maximum point of interest is Praça Luís de Camões.

It is in this square that we find the **cathedral**, a Gothic building which nevertheless also contains Manueline and Renaissance elements. In the interior is an excellent representation of the life of Jesus, carved in stone.

For their part, the **churches of A Mesicórdia and São Vicente** are excellent exponents of the baroque monuments to be found in the town.

Also of interest are the **Palaces of O Conselho** (16th century); the **castle** (12th century), a magnificent viewpoint over the city at an altitude of 1,056 metres, and the remains of a **Roman road** which testifies to the presence of this civilisation in ancient Guarda.

INTERIOR OF THE CATHEDRAL.

OVERALL VIEWS OF COIMBRA,
PORTUGAL'S THIRD CITY.

First capital of the independent Portuguese kingdom, Coimbra, now the country's third city after Lisbon and Porto, lies halfway between the two on the right bank of the River Mondego. For nearly three centuries, Coimbra shared with Lisbon the honour of being the seat of the University de Portugal, one of the oldest in Europe. The city, founded in 1290, was finally established in ancient Roman *Aeminium* by decree of King João in 1537. Its original name was changed to that of Coimbra after the destruction of the nearby township of Conimbriga, the largest human settlement established by the Romans on Lusitanian territory. The Suevians razed it in 468, and the inhabitants of *Aeminium* finally adopted and adapted its name.

The **ruins of Conimbriga**, found some 15 kilometres from Coimbra, are well-worth a detailed visit due to the importance of the site. Archaeological investigation has unearthed spectacular mosaics, thermal baths, houses, part of an aqueduct and remains of the Roman forum. Sculptures, coins, ceramic objects and other interesting items unearthed on the site are displayed in the little museum adjoining the site. This is, in short, Portugal's most important archaeological site.

Coimbra is divided into two clearly-differentiated zones. The upper part of the town, where the clergy and the nobility used to have their residences, has a markedly medieval air, whilst the lower part, the abode of artisans, traders and the rest of the population, maintains its more popular air.

There are two cathedrals in the higher part of the city. The **Sé Velha**, or Old Cathedral, built in the 12th century, is Romanesque in style and has a square ground plan. Its principal characteristics are its fortress-like aspect and simple interior. In 1772, the Episcopal see was transferred to the **Sé Nova,** or New Cathedral, built by the Jesuits in baroque style in the 16th century.

Of the **University**, the most interesting elements are the great room used for meetings and other academic acts and known as the Sala dos Capelos, an entrance doorway

THE SÉ VELHA, OR OLD CATHEDRAL EXTERIOR AND HIGH ALTAR.

THE NEW CATHEDRAL WAS BUILT IN THE 16TH CENTURY.

COIMBRA UNIVERSITY IS ONE OF THE OLDEST IN EUROPE.

to the site in Mannerist style, the Porta Férrea, and the fascinating library, which contains over 150,000 books and manuscripts, some of them of outstanding value. From the courtyard, known as the Pátio das Escolas, the visitor can enjoy magnificent panoramic views of the River Mondego and the surrounding areas of the city.

Not far from this ancient centre of education are the **Botanical Gardens** with their varied sample of tropical flora. The park dates from the 18th century and was built by the then all-powerful Marquis of Pombal.

Another of the interesting sights in this part of the city is the **Machado de Castro Museum**, which occupies the ancient seat of the Episcopal Palace. Besides numerous objects dating from the Middle Ages, the building also offers visitors the chance to explore an unusual labyrinth of galleries of Roman origin found in the basement of the building.

Some distance from the historic city centre of Coimbra is the **Monastery of Santa Cruz**, which began to be built in the 12th century at the command of King Afonso Henriques and

was considerably reformed four centuries later. Here are the tombs of this king and his son and successor, Sancho I. The predominant architectural style found here is the Manueline, featured particularly in the church, the choir and the Cloister of O Silêncio. Another outstanding element is the church pulpit, by the French sculptor Nicolás Chanterène in 1552.

If the so-called upper part of the city of Coimbra boasts two cathedrals, it must be said that the lower part has two **convents of Santa Clara**. The oldest of these, with a Gothic ground plan, was abandoned towards the end of the 17th century due to the unpredictability of the River Mondego, as it was feared it might burst its banks at any time. Just a few metres away, but in a much safer place, the new Convent of Santa Clara was built during this same period. The church of the convent houses the solid silver tomb of Queen Isabella of Aragon, patron saint of Coimbra.

Portugal in Miniature ("O Portugal dos Pequeninos") offers a quick and simple way of admiring all that is finest in the country. The park, not far from the two convents described above, constitutes a thorough tour of Portugal's architectural heritage in the form of scale reproductions.

Amongst the chief civil buildings in the city, we should mention particularly the **Quinta das Lágrimas**, a place closely-linked to the sentimental drama undergone by Inês de Castro, lover of the future Pedro I. The young prince's father, King Afonso IV, did not condone his love for Inês, however, and it would appear that the assassination of Inês de Castro was carried out by royal command.

But apart from its monuments, lower Coimbra is made up of a seductive labyrinth of streets which have sagely retained the atmosphere of by-gone times. This charm is kept alive, too, by the typical *fado*, Portugal's most representative form of musical expression. Here are several establishments where daily performances of *fado* – pure feeling – are offered. According to the experts, unlike the Lisbon *fado*, which is of more popular origins, the roots of the *fado* in Coimbra are to be found in the halls of its University.

THE CHURCH OF SANTA CRUZ, IN THE MANUELINE STYLE.

THE ALMEDINA ARCH.

AN ANGEL TWICE ANNOUNCED THE APPARITIONS OF THE VIRGIN.

The life of Lúcia, Francisco and Jacinta, three little shepherds from the village of Aljustrel, near Fátima, was never to be the same after that 13 May 1917. That Sunday, they were in a spot known as the Cave of Iria when they suddenly witnessed a strange vision. Atop an oak tree, they could make out the silhouette of a woman dressed in white and surrounded by a mantle of light. Only the oldest of the children, Lúcia, was able to speak to her. Jacinta saw and heard her, whilst her brother, Francisco, could only see her image.

These apparitions, which had been announced by an angel, were repeated over the next five months, though only at the last of them, on 13 October, did the lady reveal her identity. She was the Virgin of the Rosary who, before the awed gaze of over 70,000 people come here from all over Portugal, made the sun move for ten minutes. The phenomenon, also visible in other parts of the country, was called the "sun dance". News of these events spread like wildfire, and Fátima quickly became one of the world's most important places of Marian pilgrimage.

The first chapel for worship of the Virgin was built over the site of the apparitions in 1919. Destroyed by a bomb, the modest present construction was built three years later. The column which stands before it marks the exact spot from which the Virgin spoke to the children.

THE BELLTOWER OF THE BASILICA OF A VIRGEM DO ROSÁRIO RISES MAJESTICALLY TO A HEIGHT OF 65 METRES.

FAMILIA TORNA-TE AQUILO QUE ES

SOME PILGRIMS CROSS THE ENTIRE SQUARE ON THEIR KNEES WHILST SAYING THE ROSARY.

TWO VIEWS OF THE SANCTUARY WITH THE TINY CHAPEL OF THE APPARITIONS.

SINCE THE FIRST APPARITION ON 13 MAY 1917, THE HUNDREDS OF THOUSANDS OF THE FAITHFUL WHO FLOCK HERE EVERY YEAR HAVE MADE FÁTIMA ONE OF THE MOST IMPORTANT CENTRES OF PILGRIMAGE IN EUROPE.

THE CALVARY AND THE CHAPEL OF
THE VIA CRUCIS.

In 1928, work began on the Basilica of O Rosario, a huge church
finally consecrated on 14 May
1953. Its enormous belltower, 65
metres in height and topped by
a crown and a cross weighing
seven tonnes, dominate the
esplanade where up to some one
million people can congregate.
The central statue, of the Sacred
Heart, marks the point where the
waters of a spring flowed during
the period of the apparitions. The
sides of this immense square are

MONUMENT TO THE THREE LITTLE
SHEPHERDS, INAUGURATED ON
10 JUNE 1997.

PHOTOGRAPH OF THE THREE LITTLE SHEPHERDS, TAKEN ON 13 JULY 1917. FROM LEFT TO RIGHT, LÚCIA, FRANCISCO AND JACINTA.

THE CHAPEL ERECTED IN THE VALINHOS LOCALITY, IN MEMORY OF THE FOURTH APPARITION OF OUR LADY ON THE 19TH OF AUGUST, 1917.

closed by fine porticoes under which are represented the Stations of the Cross in majolica. The houses where the little shepherds lived are still standing in **Aljustrel**, some of the rooms even conserved just as they were at the time. Not far from the village are two other sites which daily attract large numbers of pilgrims: **Valinhos**, where the Virgin appeared for the fourth time, and **Loca do Cabeço**, where the announcing angel was seen twice.

THE HOUSE WHERE LÚCIA WAS BORN.

THE HOUSE WHERE FRANCISCO AND JACINTA WERE BORN.

Ancient seat of the Knights Templar, Tomar grew up in the shelter of its **castle** walls, built by the religious and military order in the mid-12th century. The fortress played an important role during the period when Moorish incursions were frequent in the territory stretching between the Duero and the Tagus. The keep, mute witness to past deeds of heroism, majestically presides over the entire walled site.

Nevertheless, it is the **Convent of Cristo** which receives the greatest praise for its outstanding beauty and original design. Built in the 13th century, it has a circular ground plan and houses various masterpieces of Portuguese architecture. Particularly fine is the Chapter House window, an authentic compendium of Manueline art; the Charola, a small Romanesque church reminiscent of the Holy Sepulchre in Jerusalem; and the Cloister of Os Filipes, where Philip II of Spain was proclaimed king of Portugal. UNESCO listed the Convent of Cristo de Tomar as World Heritage in 1983.

CONVENT OF CRISTO: CHOIR AND CLOISTER OF OS FILIPES.

PARTIAL VIEW OF NAZARÉ FROM O SÍTIO.

According to legend, in 1182 a nobleman from nearby Porto de Mos almost fell from a cliff whilst attempting to hunt a deer on horseback. With the abyss opening up at his feet, the man commended himself to the Virgin before finally managing to halt his steed's frenetic pacing. In his gratitude, the nobleman decided to build a hermitage in honour of his saviour. This tale explaining the foundation of Nazaré is reproduced in images in mosaics decorating the walls of the tiny sanctuary.

What is certainly history and offers no doubts as to its veracity is that the first dwellers in this lovely town – now devoted to tourism – made their living from fishing. This seafaring spirit still imbues the town, with its white buildings and numerous enchanting spots.

Nazaré is divided into two clearly-differentiated zones. That known as **O Sítio**, the original core of the town, lies at the top of the cliff, 110 metres above sea level, majestically dominating the entire bay. Besides the **hermitage**, this area also contains the **Church of O Sítio**, which houses a carving of the Virgin made in Nazaré, where the mother of Jesus was born.

A funicular railway links O Sítio and **Praia de Nazaré**, the most modern part of the town, with a full range of tourist facilities. Particularly interesting here is the **fish exchange**, or *lota*, where lively auctions take place each day when the catch is brought in, and the **Doctor Joaquin Manso Ethnological Museum**, with its collections of articles relating to the world of fishing.

The origins of the magnificent **Monastery de Santa Maria da Vitória** – listed as World Heritage by UNESCO in 1983 – are to be found in King João I's prayers before the Battle of Aljubarrota in 1385. Having defeated the Spanish army, the king ordered the construction of this monumental site, an enormous work not completed until almost two hundred years later, for which reason the monastery features a combination of various architectural styles. Nevertheless, the building is rightly considered one of the finest exponents of Portuguese Gothic, though with a significant number of Manueline elements.

The main front, an excellent example of the Flamboyant Gothic, is decorated with figures representing personages from the Old Testament. The interior is divided into a nave and two aisles of astounding height. The right aisle leads to the Chapel of O Fundador, where João I and his wife are buried. The other side communicates with the lovely royal cloister, ornamented in Manueline style. Also interesting are the Imperfect Chapels, thus known because they were never completed as can be seen, for example, in the vault which should cover them but was never finished. The entrance is formed by a splendid portal dating from the early-16th century.

The tiny town of A Batalha, somewhat eclipsed by the fame and beauty of its monastery, grew up due to the arrival of countless artists and labourers who came here to take part in the gigantic enterprise. The town still conserves several of the houses built in those times.

MONASTERY OF SANTA MARIA DA VITÓRIA.

THE TOMBS OF JOÃO I AND PHILIPPA OF LANCASTER.

THE ROYAL ▶ CLOISTER, OR CLOISTER OF JOÃO I, EXEMPLIFIES THE MAGNIFICENT RESULTS OBTAINED FROM THE COMBINATION OF THE GOTHIC AND MANUELINE STYLES.

THE GOTHIC CLOISTER OF THE ROYAL ABBEY OF SANTA MARIA IS THE LARGEST IN PORTUGAL IN THIS ARCHITECTURAL STYLE.

The **Royal Abbey of Santa Maria**, a 12th-century monastery pertaining to the Cistercian order and listed as World Heritage by UNESCO in 1989, is the reason why the name of the tiny town of Alcobaça is so well-known internationally. Tradition links the name of the abbey to the first Portuguese monarch. Apparently, Afonso Henriques conceded the land to enable the monks of this order to take up residence in Portugal. The sum of the two wills gave fruit in the form of what is considered an outstanding example of early Goth-

ic architecture. Only the front of the church, which has been successively altered, escapes from the austerity of the decoration and the simplicity of the forms characterising the interior. The church, with ground plan in the form of a Latin cross, is, at 106 metres, the longest in the country. At the ends of the transept lie the mortal remains of Pedro I and his ill-starred lover, Inês de Castro. Their tombs constitute magnificent examples of medieval funerary art.

The main cloister, dedicated to King Dinis and known as the Cloister of

Silence, is the largest gothic cloister in Portugal, its austerity the key to much of its serene beauty. The upper storey was added in Manueline style at a later date.

The courtyard communicates with the kitchen, presided over by an unusual chimney adorned with 13th-century glazed tiles. Branching off from the cloister we also find the refectory, a magnificent room with three vaulted aisles, and the Royal Room (Sala dos Reis), where the glazed tiles on the walls illustrate the history of the foundation of the monastery.

THE 12TH-CENTURY WALLS WHICH STILL TODAY ENCIRCLE THE TOWN OF ÓBIDOS IN THEIR EMBRACE.

The lovely town of Óbidos, probably one of the best-conserved medieval cities in all Portugal, is embraced by the walls of a 12th-century **castle**. Of the many pages which go to form the book of its history, the most outstanding is that which speaks of its connections to royal weddings. Over the period between the 13th and 19th centuries, Óbidos formed part of the dowry which Portuguese kings gave their wives on the occasion of their marriage. To

THE CHURCH OF SANTA MARIA.

judge by the charm of the place, this gift must without doubt have been received with great joy by all those entering into holy wedlock.

Of the four gates which were once opened up in the thick walls, the main one is the south gate. Entering the town through this corridor, the visitor finds that Óbidos is an endless compendium of monuments, mansions, winding streets and nooks and corners reminiscent of other periods. Amongst the most important of the town's monuments are the **Church of Santa Maria**, whose origins go back to the period of Visigoth rule; the **Church of São Pedro**, with its find baroque altarpiece; and the **Church of Santiago**, once the castle chapel. Beyond the walls is the **Sanctuary of O Senhor Jesus da Pedra**, a much-visited church where, according to tradition, many miracle cures have taken place.

STREETS OF ÓBIDOS.

Due to its privileged situation, the city of Santarém, capital of the fertile Ribatejo county, served for many years as a trade and military filter for neighbouring Lisbon. Known to the Romans as *Scallabis*, the present name goes back to the Visigoth period and reflects the inhabitants' fervent devotion to Saint Iria or Irene. The many white houses of the city stand out in an urban layout whose design reminds us that the Moorish armies were stationed here for many years.

Also known as the "Capital of the Gothic", Santarém boasts many outstanding buildings making the city well worth a visit. The **Church of Graça**, which houses the tomb of the discoverer of Brazil, Pedro Álvares Cabral, does full honour to that architectural style. Also interesting is the **Church of São João de Alporão**, built during the transition between Romanesque and Gothic and now the seat of the **Archaeological Museum**.

Finally, we should mention the **Portas do Sol park**, at one end of the city, where remains of the old city walls are still conserved, and which also commands magnificent views over Ribatejo county, the River Tagus and surrounding towns and villages.

THE AUSTERE INTERIOR OF THE CHURCH OF GRAÇA.

THE CHURCH OF SÃO JOÃO DE ALPORÃO.

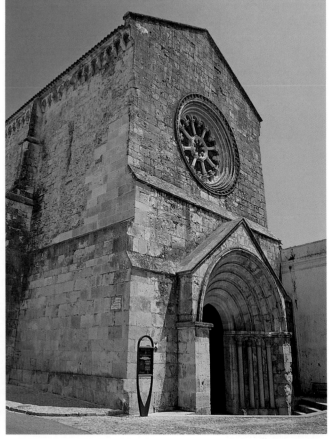

THE MONASTERY OF MAFRA HAS 800 ROOMS AND DORMITORIES.

This tiny village near Lisbon is made remarkable by its monastery of large proportions, built in the 18th century in accordance with a vote taken by João V. The construction of this imposing building, 40,000 square metres in area, began in 1711, after it was announced that the queen consort, Maria Ana of Austria, was expecting a baby. The Portuguese ruler had promised to build this great monument if his wife could give him an heir. The economic boom in the country over the following years enabled the monastery to be extended to its present proportions. Some 45,000 workers were employed on this enormous undertaking, and materials were brought here from as far afield as Brazil and Italy.

VIEW OF THE BASILICA TRANSEPT.

ROYAL PALACE OF QUELUZ: THRONE ROOM.

One of the most outstanding works of Portuguese architecture lies in the outskirts of Queluz: the **Palácio Real**, or Royal Palace, former residence of the Portuguese monarchs, built in the 18th century by the architects Mateus Vicente and Jean Baptiste Robillon. Sumptuous and of enormous proportions, the palace is also known as the Portuguese Versailles due to its clearly French influence, evident in its forms, interiors and, above all, carefully-tended gardens. Particularly attractive is the Garden of Neptune, separated from the rest by a balustrade crowned by statues by Manuel Alves and Silvestre de Faria.

In the interior, of particular interest is the Louis XV-style Throne Room, used for long sessions of music and dance. Similarly beautiful, the walls of the Ambassadors' Room are adorned with fine paintings, marbles and mirrors. The King's Chamber, also known as that of Don Quijote, is decorated by paintings illustrating different episodes in the adventures of that singular Spanish knight, whilst the ceiling of the State Council Chamber features a magnificent pictorial allegory on the theme of time. Our tour of the interior of the Royal Palace of Queluz is completed by a visit to the house known as the Casa das Mangas, its walls adorned by glazed tiles reproducing scenes from Portuguese voyages of discovery; the Merendas Room, with 18th-century paintings; the Oratory of Princesses Maria José and Maria Doroteia; the Lanternem Room, which contains a painting of King Michael; and the Music Room, with three spectacular Venetian glass candelabrums.

ROYAL PALACE OF SINTRA.

The outstandingly beautiful city of Sintra stands on a small massif forming part of the sierra of the same name. Sintra, once the summer residence of Portuguese monarchs nobles, was declared World Heritage by UNESCO in 1995. The landscape around the city also helps to highlight the personality and charm of this city, which has awoken passions and been the object of passionate elegies by poets and writers such as Camões and Lord Byron.

At the top of the mountain perch the remains of the so-called **Moorish Castle**, built in the 8th century and the finest example of Moorish military architecture conserved in Portugal.

Another of Sintra's jewels is the **Palace of A Pena**, considered to be the outstanding masterpiece of Portuguese Romanticism. The palace, which lies in the most idyllic of settings, was built thanks to the artistic sensitivity of Ferdinand II, who in the mid-19th century commissioned the German architect Ludwig von Eschwege to design the palace and recover an old 16th-century Hieronymites' monastery, which stands on this same site. The result features a combination of various styles – Egyptian, Oriental, Gothic, Manueline and Renaissance – which exist side-by-side in surprising harmony and beauty. The colours it now sports, the result of recent restoration, even further accentuates the feeling of being in an enchanted castle.

No less surprising is the park known as the **Parque da Pena**, also designed by von Eschwege with the aim of providing a suitable backdrop for his splendid palace. To this end, the local trees where replaced by

examples of more exotic species, fountains were built and waters rechannelled. The fruit of all this work is now one of the best-conserved wonders of Portugal.

In the heart of old Sintra is the Palácio Real, or **Royal Palace**, which began to be built in the 14th century and was successively extended over the years. Besides its splendid architectural style, impregnated with Oriental elements, the Royal Palace also boasts the most important collection of Mudéjar glazed tiles in the country.

Also of outstanding beauty and interest is the **Seteais Palace**, built in the 18th century and converted into an hotel in 1954, and the **Monserrate Palace and Park**, another example of Romantic architecture set in the most spectacular natural surroundings.

MOORISH CASTLE WALLS.

THE PALACE OF A PENA.

THE GARDENS OF THE PALACE OF MONTSERRATE HOUSE EXTREMELY BEAUTIFUL NOOKS.

VIEW OF THE POPULAR ALFAMA DISTRICT.

Elegant, welcoming and modern, the capital of Portugal gazes at its own reflection in the waters of the Tagus from the seven hills on which it lies. Just a few kilometres before it merges forever into the ocean, and having previously crossed the entire country, the river's course broadens out as it passes through the city, forming a great estuary. The golden brushstrokes dabbed on the water's surface by the sun has made this curious river widening known under the name of the "Sea of Straw".

Lisbon's river port has played an important role in the life of the country since time immemorial. Many Mediterranean peoples came to it, attracted by the trade potential of its privileged position. To one of these, the Phoenicians, is attributed in 800 BC the foundation of *Alis Ubbo* or *Olissipo*, names from which the present name of Lisbon derive. The Romans occupied the city some five centuries later, and it was Julius Caesar who baptised it as *Felicitas Julia*. Later, various Vandal tribes settled here in the 5th and 6th centuries before the Visigoths finally established a short period of peace and stability which was broken by the Moorish invasion in the year 714. The labyrinthine distribution of its streets and the prefix "al" show the Alfama district to be a mute witness to the period of Arab domination.

In 1147, Afonso Henriques, at the head of a large force of crusaders

whose ultimate destination was the Holy Land, reconquered the city for Christianity. Four years previously, this grandson of King Alfonso VI of León had been proclaimed the first king of Portugal. Having taken Lisbon, Afonso Henriques set about consolidating the identity of the new kingdom which had begun to take shape in the duchy of Portucale, north of the River Mondego. A century later, in 1255, Lisbon replaced Coimbra as the capital of Portugal.

The 15th and 16th centuries were one of the most prosperous periods in the history of the city, coinciding with the reign of the Avis dynasty. It was under the patronage of these monarchs that the great sea voyages of discovery were undertaken that where to make the country a world power and Lisbon a strategic point on trade routes.

On 1 November 1755 a great earthquake shook the city, killing many – some estimates speak of as many as 60,000 dead of a population of 270,000 – and devastated the centre of the city. The Marquis of Pombal, King José I's Secretary of State and a fervent follower of enlightened rationalism, order its reconstruction with the application of new town planning criteria which over the coming years were to become generally adopted throughout Europe. The width and rectilinear layout of streets, wide spaces and the uniformity of buildings are the most characteristic features of the reconstruction plan drawn up by Pombal.

The population explosion of the mid-19th century prompted the construction of the railway here, as well as the installation of the city's first

AERIAL VIEW OF PRAÇA DO IMPÉRIO.

public lighting system. This period also saw the establishment of the bases of the present city, with the construction of such great avenues as Avenida la Liberdade and Avenida Nova.

Three great key mark the history of Lisbon in the 20th century. The first was the opening in 1966 of the 25 de abril bridge, which broke the hundred-year isolation of the south bank. The second was a fire in 1988 which devastated O Chiado, one of the city's

ROSSIO STATION, A FINE EXAMPLE OF THE MANUELINE STYLE.

PRAÇA DA FIGUEIRA.

most emblematic neighbourhoods. Finally, the opportunity represented by the hosting of the Universal Exhibition in 1998 was seized to carry out an ambitious plan to regenerate the eastern part of the city.

The heart of Portugal's capital is the popular **Praça do Rossio** in La Baixa neighbourhood, the meeting-point of locals and visitors alike, and a visit not to be missed. The real name of this square is Praça Dom Pedro IV, after the country's first constitutional king whose statue presides over this emblematic site. The cafés, shops and flower stalls of the square compose an attractive setting and an invitation visitors to slow their pace and take time to drink in the atmosphere. The most outstanding building in the square is the **Teatro Nacional D. Maria II**. Neo-classical in style, this was once the headquarters of the Inquisition, or Holy Office. The sentences passed down by this institution were read out in the nearby **Church of São Domingos**, built in the 13th century and partially destroyed in the 1755 earthquake. On the opposite side of the square is **O Rossio Station**, a fine example of what has become known as the neo-Manueline style, popular in the dying years of the 19th century.

Near O Rossio, **Praça da Figueira** was once the setting for one of the most important markets in Lisbon. Here, on a marble based, rises majestically the equestrian statue of João I, the first ruler under the Avis dynasty.

Rua Augusta joins Praça do Rossio with Praça do Comércio, a enormous square whose spaciousness is enhanced by its harmonious architecture. The square is also known as Terreiro do Paço as the Palácio Nacional, or National Palace, stood here before it was destroyed by the 1755 earthquake. In the centre is the monument to King José I (1775), which reminds us that the reconstruction of the city began under his reign. Three sides of this square are occupied by porticoed buildings, whilst the south side looks out over the River Tagus from a lovely staircase reminiscent of Venice. To the north, the Arch of Triumph, in Louis XIV style, communicates with the main thoroughfares of Lisbon.

AERIAL VIEW OF PRAÇA DO COMÉRCIO AND BAIXA DISTRICT.

If this neighbourhood, A Baixa, is characterised by the rational design of its urban network, just a few steps away, the **O Chiado** neighbourhood offers a completely different appearance, with its labyrinth of narrow streets and tiny squares. This picturesque area was devastated by fire in 1988, when many of the luxurious shops here were completely destroyed.

Bairro Alto is a district comprising a succession of steep streets which, like the Alfama neighbourhood, was left practically unscathed by the 1755 earthquake.

Built in the 17th century, this is now one of the principal centres of night life in Lisbon, due to its many taverns, from which flow interminably the rhythmic notes of the popular *fado*. The **Santa Justa Lift** is one

THE SANTA JUSTA LIFT.

THE CONVENT OF O CARMO.

of the easiest ways of travelling from one level to another in this steep quarter of the city. The lift, built by Portuguese engineer Raúl Mesnier du Ponsard, a follower of the famed Eiffel, travels a vertical distance of 32 metres, though it reaches a total height of 45. Neo-Gothic in style, it was officially opened and entered into service in 1902.

Standing near the lift, the **Convent of O Carmo** is considered the most precious jewel in Lisbon's Gothic crown. It was built between the late-14th century and the early-15th at the command of Nuno Álvares Pereira as a sign of gratitude to the Virgin for the victory won over Spanish forces by the Portuguese at the Battle of Aljubarrota. The convent interior, badly damaged in the 18th century by the earthquake, houses a small but interesting archaeological museum containing a valuable collection of sculptures, engravings, tombs and escutcheons.

In contrast to the austerity of the Convent of O Carmo, certain of the chapels in the **Church of São Roque** contain the largest number of decorative element to be found anywhere in Lisbon. Built by the Jesuits in the late-16th century, its most outstanding elements are the Chapel of São João Baptista, a neo-classical work in gold, silver, ivory and Carrara marble; the High Chapel, with its magnificent altarpiece; and the Chapel of Santo António, adorned with baroque and neo-classical paintings and carvings. Beside the church, the **Museum of Sacred Art** contains a large collection of reliquaries, pre-

BASILICA OF A ESTRELA.

THE HIERYONIMITES' MONASTERY, A VERITABLE JEWEL OF MANUELINE ART.

cious metal work and Renaissance painting.

Nearby, not far from the **Palace of São Bento**, a former Benedictine convent which was rebuilt according to neo-classical canons towards the end of the 19th century, is the **Basilica Of A Estrela**. Also known as the Basilica of the Heart of Jesus, the building, in rococo style though with neo-classical elements, takes its inspiration from the layout of the Convent of Mafra. Its imposing façade is composed of two towers and a two-storey dome. Inside are the tombs of Saint Exuperio and Queen Maria, at whose command the sanctuary was built in the late-18th century.

Just a few streets away is the **Palace of As Necessidades**, the official residence of the kings of Portugal from its construction in the mid-18th century to the abolition of the monarchy in 1910. It is now the seat of the Ministry of Foreign Affairs. Many of the art works which once adorned the palace are now housed in museums all over the country and in the Ajuda, Queluz and Sintra palaces.

The **National Palace of Ajuda**, also a former royal residence, is now used for occasional institutional acts of the Presidency of the Republic. Built in the early-19th century, it contains three dining-rooms, an interesting library founded by the Marquis of Pombal and a museum with over 30 exhibition rooms featuring part of the luxurious furnishings which formerly pertained to the Portuguese monarchy.

The palace surroundings are presided over by the so-called **Tapada de Ajuda**, a spacious park of some 200 hectares where King José I used to hunt.

Another of Lisbon's most notable monuments is also found in this western part of the city. This is the **Hie-**

ALL THE FANTASY OF MANUELINE ART IS BROUGHT SPLENDIDLY TOGETHER IN THE CLOISTER OF THE HIERYONIMITES' MONASTERY.

ronymites Monastery, a masterpiece of Manueline art built in the early-16th century employing some of the treasure Vasco de Gama brought back from his overseas expeditions. The Manueline style, which emerged during the reign of Manuel I – from whence its name – is Portugal's most representative architectural style. The style embraces the period of transition from the Gothic to the Renaissance, although its principal characteristic is its use of ornaments whose inspiration comes from the lands visited by Portuguese expeditionary forces.

This great work, initially designed by the French architect Boytac continued after his death by the Portuguese architect João de Castilho, was listed as World Heritage by UNESCO in 1983.

The enormous and outstandingly beautiful south portico, facing the Tagus, consists of two parts. The bas-reliefs in the tympanum illustrate scenes from the life of Saint Hieronymus. The interior, formed by a single nave, is a demonstration of the degree of fantasy and creativity Manueline art could reach. Filled with light and space, the church contains

the tombs of Vasco de Gama, the Discoverer, and of Luís de Camões, the great Portuguese poet, author of *Os Lusiadas*. Also interesting is the sacristy, with its single central column supporting the vault, and the high chapel, with an altarpiece reproducing scenes from the Passion of Christ. Special mention must also be made of the great cloister, a masterpiece of astounding decorative exuberance and architectural fantasy. Divided into two stories and with the unusual feature that there do not exist two identical columns in the entire site, we find here a combination of

INTERIOR
OF THE
HIERYONIMITES'
MONASTERY.

THE NAVAL MUSEUM IS HOUSED IN THE MONASTERY SITE.

magnificent Plateresque, Manueline and Renaissance ornaments. There is a predominance of celestial globes and the letter M, personal symbols of King Manuel I, as well as floral and religious motifs and different medallions.

The west wing of the monastery houses the **National Museum of Archaeology and Ethnology**, transferred here in 1903. Since its foundation, the museum has played a leading role, both nationally and internationally, in scientific research carried

THE BELÉM CULTURAL CENTRE CONTAINS TWO CONCERT HALLS AND FOUR EXHIBITION ROOMS.

THE BELÉM TOWER.

out in the fields of archaeology and ethnology. The museum rooms contain interesting collections of Egyptian antiques, African art, mosaics, stamps and medals, as well as an outstanding exhibition of Portuguese precious metal work dating from 3000 BC to the Middle Ages.

The other great museum situated in the monastery is the **Naval Museum** which, besides models of vessels of all kind and other classical elements of navigation, also contains a room housing the royal galleys used to transport illustrious visitors to the city from their boats anchored off the coast, as well as the first flying boat to cross the South Atlantic.

Just a step or two away from the monastery are two more jewels of Manueline art: the first of these is the **Bethlehem Tower** (Torre de Belém), built in the middle of the river between 1515 and 1521. Its original function was to control the access of shipping to the city. Some years later, during the Spanish occupation, it was converted into a prison. The site, of harmoniously-balanced proportions, is made up of a bastion with a hexagonal base, a cylindrical turret at each of its six corners, and the quadrangular tower itself, four stories in height. UNESCO listed this tiny, ancient old fort as World Heritage in 1983.

Near the Bethlehem Tower is the 52-metre-high **Monument to the Discoveries**, by which the city of Lisbon renders homage to all the Portuguese who took part in the great sea voyages of the 15th and 16th

MONUMENT TO CRISTO-REI AND THE APRIL 25 BRIDGE.

centuries. It was completed in 1960 and, like the Bethlehem Tower, its design recalls the prow of a boat. The figure holding a small caravel represents Prince Enrique the Navigator, accompanied by 21 illustrious personages who also rose to fame during the period of the discoveries.

From the **25 de Abril bridge**, built in 1966 by the same company which built the world-famous Golden Gate and Bay bridges in San Francisco –hence the similarities between the three– the visitor can enjoy some of the finest views to be obtained in the entire city. The bridge is two and a half kilometres long and rises to a maximum height of 60 metres over the Tagus. Its construction, satisfying a long-standing demand by the people of Lisbon, gave the Portuguese capital an enormous boost, breaking the isolation of the south bank. Besides this, the 25 de abril bridge also provides access to the beaches in Caparica, one of the holiday resorts best-loved of the people of Lisbon.

On the south bank of the river rises majestically the statue of **Cristo Rei**, 28 metres in height. The image stands on an 82-metre-high pedestal of functional lines. Inaugurated in 1959, the terrace, reached by a lift, commands breath-taking views over the city and environs.

Taking O Rossio as our point of reference, the districts to the east contain some of the oldest and most emblematic of the monuments of Lisbon. Here stands **St. George's Castle**, for instance, the veritable cradle of Lisbon, standing on the highest promontory in the city. The strategic value of this hill persuaded the Romans to build their first walls here, though the walls we now see bear

ST GEORGE'S CASTLE, SEEN FROM THE ELEVADOR DE SANTA JUSTA LIFT.

the unmistakable mark of the Moors. After the Christian reconquest, the castle was converted into a royal residence, which purpose it served in the 14th and 15th centuries, with the construction of new palaces. The different additions and alterations made in very different periods combine to give the site a unique charm. The castle still preserves the old sentry path and several towers and bastions, which now form excellent viewpoints over the most ancient areas of Lisbon.

One of these neighbourhoods is the **Alfama** district, a labyrinth of narrow streets, tiny squares and staircases whose origins go back to Visigoth times, though its final layout is the work of the Moors. Once rich in hot water fountains, the Arabs gave it the name of "al-hamma", meaning, precisely, "thermal waters". Until the 1755 earthquake, many rich Lisbon families lived in this part of the city, which is at its loveliest during the festivities in honour of the patron saint of the city in mid-June.

ALFAMA TYPICAL STREET.

LISBON
CATHEDRAL,
WITH ITS
IMPRESSIVE
ASPECT OF A
FORTRESS.

THE CHURCH OF SANTO ANTÓNIO.

In the opinion of many, it is in Alfama that the *fado* acquires its maximum expression. The finest interpretations of this popular song can be heard in some of the fishermen's taverns which dot these streets of leaning houses.

At one of the exits from this peculiar labyrinth, the visitor almost unexpectedly comes upon **Lisbon Cathedral**. The cathedral, or Sé, is an imposing building with the appearance of a fortress which harmoniously combines the Romanesque and Gothic styles. It began to be built in the mid-12th century after the troops of King Afonso Henriques conquered the city from the Moors. The more recent elements which the visitor will observe in it are the consequence of restoration carried out after the earthquakes of 1385 and 1755. A rose window crowns the simple doorway, which is flanked by two powerful towers. The interior, with a Latin cross ground plan, contains the Gothic Chapel of Bartolomeu Joanes, in which is a splendid baroque altarpiece, the tombs of King Afonso IV and his wife in the high altar, and the cloister, which retains its magical medieval air in spite of suffering serious damage from earthquakes.

The **Church of Santo António** stands just a few metres from the Sé. It was built in the late-18th century in honour of Saint Anthony, the most venerated saint in Lisbon. The church crypt stands, according to tradition, on the site of the house where Saint Anthony was born in 1195.

FRONT OF THE HOUSE KNOWN AS THE CASA DOS BICOS.

FRONT OF THE CHURCH OF SÃO VICENTE DE FORA.

In nearby Rua dos Bacalhoeiros, or "cod-sellers street", stands one of the city's most singular buildings. This is the palace known as the **Casa dos Bicos** ("House of Points"), thus known for the profusion of stones cut, according to some, in pyramid shape and, according to others, in diamond shape, and which decorate the front. The palace, built in the 16th century, is a notable example of the Portuguese Gothic style.

The **Church of São Vicente de Fora**, also located in this area, was built at the command of Philip II in 1582 on the site of an earlier church also devoted to Saint Vincent. Since the original building lay outside the boundaries of medieval Lisbon, it was known as "de Fora" ("outside"). The church was designed by the Italian architect Filippo Terzzi who, following Renaissance canon, took his inspiration from Romanesque churches of the period. The front has three porticoes and twin belltowers, whilst the interior, with a single nave, has a Latin cross ground plan. Particu-

THE SANTA ENGRÁCIA CHURCH-PANTHEON.

larly interesting are the magnificent baroque high altar and the two cloisters decorated with 18th-century glazed tiles.

Campo de Santa Engrácia joins this church with the **Church-Pantheon of Santa Engrácia**, one of the finest exponents of Portuguese baroque architecture. Originally designed as a church in the 17th century, alterations carried out in the mid-20th converted it into a pantheon for the eternal rest of illustrious personages. The constant repair and conversion work carried out on the building prompted the local people to coin

the saying "the work of Santa Engrácia", used to refer to an event or undertaking which appears interminable. The most striking elements in this imposing marble building on its base in the form of a Greek cross, are the dome and the terrace roof, which commands splendid views of the surrounding area.

The popular fair known as the **Feria da Ladra**, the oldest in the city, has been held near the churches of São Vicente and Santa Engrácia every Tuesday and Saturday since 1882. This flea market, whose origins appear to go back to the period of

the Christian Reconquest, converts the whole area into a busy hive of activity as potential purchasers inspect the huge variety of goods on offer.

The most modern part of Lisbon lies in the eastern zone. On the occasion of the hosting of the Universal Exhibition in 1998, an ambitious town planning project was implemented, radically transforming the very physiognomy of the urban landscape. To this end, a refinery, an abattoir, a refuse dump and various army warehouses were demolished to make way for a new residential district,

THE LADRA FAIR, THE OLDEST OF ALL THOSE HELD IN LISBON.

THE VASCO DA GAMA BRIDGE IS 16 KILOMETRES IN LENGTH.

the **Oriente Station** (East Station) and the magnificent new **Vasco da Gama bridge**. Legacies of this same great event are the Pavilion of the Oceans, now one of the largest **oceanariums** in the world, the **Portugal Pavilion**, work of Álvaro Siza, and the **Atlantic Pavilion**.

The modern **Oriente Station**, where rail, bus and metro transport networks converge, is the work of the Spanish architect Santiago Calatrava. In an allusion to the many trees in the city of Lisbon, the design of the metallic roof sup-

THE PAVILION OF THE OCEANS, BUILT ON THE OCCASION OF THE UNIVERSAL EXHIBITION IN 1998.

THE ORIENTE STATION.

ports of this steel and glass building themselves resemble so many branches.

The construction of **Vasco da Gama bridge** constituted an important improvement to Lisbon's road network. The bridge has a total length of 16 kilometres, of which thirteen are over the waters of the River Tagus. These figures make it one of the longest bridges in the world.

But Lisbon is also gardens and viewpoints, not to mention museums. Situated in Eduardo VII park, the **Estufa Fria** is a tropical garden officially opened in 1930, though built 20

THE EDUARDO VII PARK.

THE "ESTUFA FRIA" GARDENS.

years previously. Here grow local botanical species alonside others from warmer and wetter climes. With a jungle structure, the natural landscape is criss-crossed by zigzagging paths leading to grottoes, pools, waterfalls and other nooks and crannies of outstanding beauty and interest.

For its part, the **Botanical Garden** is also home to many plants from different latitudes. With its 2,500 different species, this is considered one of the finest of its type in Europe.

OVERALL VIEW OF LISBON FROM ST. GEORGE'S CASTLE.

These two gardens, set out at the top of their respective hills, command fine views over the city. Other spectacular viewpoints over the city include those of **São Pedro de Alcântara**, near the Bairro Alto, **Santa Luzia**, near St. George's Castle, and **Santa Catarina**, which dominates the entire city.

Turning now to the principal museums in the city, besides the Naval and Archaeological museums, described above, we should also mention the Decorative Arts, Ancient Art, Carriage, Military, Gulbenkian and Glazed Tile museums.

The collections of the **Museum of Decorative Arts**, housed in the Azurara Palace (17th century), are composed of period furniture, precious metal work, ancient engravings and ceramics.

The **Museum of Ancient Art** is considered the most important in Portugal. The building which houses it, a 17th-century palace near the docks, is popularly known as "Janelas verdes" ("green blinds"). The works featured include, particularly, "The Temptations of Saint Anthony", one of Hieronymus Bosch's most famous paintings; Holbein's "The Fountain of Life"; Dürer's "Saint Jerome"; various paintings by Velázquez and Ribera, and a magnificent collection of works by Portuguese artists, particularly Nuno Gonçalves and the panels making up the famed "Polyptich of Saint Vincent".

The royal carriages of Philip I and João V are two of the most valuable pieces in the **Carriage Museum**, one of the most important of its kind in the world.

The **Military Museum** provides an interesting review of the uniforms and arms of the Portuguese army from the 18th to the 20th centuries.

VIEW FROM THE SANTA LUZIA VIEWPOINT.

For its part, the **Gulbenkian Museum** is just a part of the foundation created by the oil magnate to house a truly outstanding art collection, some of which go as far back as 2800 BC. The legacy of Calouste Gulbenkian has been displayed in a modern building in Avenida de Berna

THE MUSEUM OF DECORATIVE ARTS.

ONE OF THE ROOMS IN THE CARRIAGE MUSEUM.

since 1969, when the museum was inaugurated. Its many rooms contain both classical and oriental works from Egypt, Syria and the Far East; and European art, featuring statues by Rodin and paintings by Degas, Monet, Renoir and Rembrandt, amongst others.

A library, several exhibition and conference rooms and a modern art centre complete the cultural facilities contained in this museum, now the property of the Portuguese State in

THE GULBENKIAN MUSEUM.

accordance with the desire expressed by Gulbenkian before his death.

The **Glazed Tile Museum** (Museu dos Azulejos) is housed in the Convent of A Madre de Deus, a building founded in 1509 by Leonor, widow of João II and sister of King Manuel. The entire site is profusely decorated with lavish glazed tiles, though the museum proper is contained in a number of rooms around the splendid two-storeyed cloister. Beginning with examples of ancient pieces from Granada, Seville and Manises, the exhibition comprises a complete review of the development and history of the glazed tile in Portugal.

BENFICA FOOTBALL STADIUM: SHOW BY THE CLUB MASCOT, VITÓRIA, AND OVERALL VIEW.

CASCAIS CLIFF, BETTER KNOWN AS THE BOCAS DO INFERNO ("MOUTHS OF HELL").

Around three kilometres from Estoril, overlooking a splendid bay, Cascais is another old fishing village which has become one of Portugal's most important tourist resorts in recent years. As far back as the period from 1870 to 1910, in fact, the Portuguese monarchs chose Cascais to spend the summer months, a custom continued by various presidents of the Portuguese Republic. Proof of this are the many little palaces found in a town which has wisely harmonised its historic legacy with the development of a modern tourist industry. Amongst the historic buildings in Cascais, the most outstanding is the **citadel**, which dates from the 17th century and dominates the entire coastline from the top of the hill. The walls of this citadel still conserve sections going back to ancient times. Also interesting are the **Church of Nossa Senhora da Assunção**, also built in the 17th century, though reformed in the 20th; the **Church of Os Navegantes**, a simple example of baroque art; and the English-style **Palace of the Dukes of Palmela**. Nature has also made an important contribution to the beauty of Cascais, regaling it with spectacular cliffs known as the **Mouths of Hell**. Situated one kilometre from the town centre, these cliffs contain various caves communicating with the sea. The beating of the waves against this immense rock wall causes an awe-inspiring noise which eloquently explains the name given to the site by the local people.

Its temperate climate, comparable with that enjoyed by the inhabitants of the South of France, and its proximity to Lisbon, from which it is separated by a distance of just 22 kilometres, provided the ingredients to convert Estoril into a tourist resort of the first order. The urban growth of this old fishing village took place around the local **Casino**, one of the most famous in Europe. The town boasts the most comfortable and modern hotel facilities which, along with its beaches, attract thousands of visitors to Estoril every year. In the environs of the town are the **prehistoric caves of Alapraia**, a necropolis whose origins go back to the transition period between the Stone and Metal ages. It would appear that the four caves forming the site were used not only as a cemetery but also as a place to store wood and a refuge for cattle. Most of the objects found at the Alapraia site are now displayed in the Museum of the Counts of Castro Guimarães in Cascais.

ESTORIL, AN OLD FISHING VILLAGE, IS NOW AN IMPORTANT TOURIST RESORT.

THE WALLED ENCLOSURE OF SETÚBAL WAS BUILT AT THE COMMAND OF PHILIP I.

Setúbal, another important summer resort near Lisbon, is an industrial and fishing city lying at the mouth of the River Sado. Its most interesting monuments include the **Church of Jesus**, the work of the same architect who designed the Hieronymites' Monastery. The building, which combines the Gothic with elements of Manueline art, features an interesting marble portal. In the interior are fine glazed tiles dating from the 17th century. The attractions of Setúbal also include the **Church of São Julião**, dating originally from the 16th century, and the **fort,** also built during the 16th century at the command of Philip I to guard the coast from pirate attacks.

DOORWAY OF THE CHURCH OF JESUS.

With its magnificent beaches and famed for its succulent tuna and swordfish dishes, Sesimbra is a tiny fishing village which has become a tourist resort of the first order over recent years. Besides the public fish auction, a truly picturesque spectacle, Sesimbra also offers such attractions as its 17th-century **castle**, now a national monument, built on the site of an old walled enclosure dating from the late-12th century. Also interesting is the **parish church**, which contains a series of pictorial representations of the popular festivity of Our Lady of the Wounds (Nossa Senhora das Chagas), a tradition going back to the 17th century.

THE CASTLE AND THE PORT OF SESIMBRA.

ELVAS: THE TEMPRE DOOR.

Close to the frontier with Spain, Elvas lies in the middle of a plain in the Alto Alentejo region. This is a city surrounded by great **walls**, splendidly conserved, which speak for themselves of the past importance of Elvas as a military stronghold. Its houses cluster along narrow little streets which, like the castle, bear the unmistakable mark of Moorish influence. The most outstanding monument here is the **Amoreira aqueduct**, seven kilometres in length. Despite its age –it was built between 1498 and 1622– it continues to operate even today. Also of interest are various religious buildings: the **cathedral**, the **churches of A Consolação**, **Nossa Senhora de la Assunção** and **Nosso Senhor Jesus da Piedade**, all adorned with fine 18th- and 19th-century glazed tiles.

Near Elvas is the city of **Estremoz**, another historic defensive bastion with castle and city walls. Estremoz is particularly famed for its ceramic products (principally jugs and cooking pots) decorated with marble encrustation from the nearby quarries.

THE AMOREIRA AQUEDUCT.

CONVENT OF OS LÓIOS.

The city of Évora, capital of the Alto Alentejo region and listed as World Heritage by UNESCO, boasts a practically uninterrupted succession of monuments and buildings of the highest artistic and historic value which make this one of the most beautiful cities in Portugal. The city originally grew up around the **Roman temple**, probably devoted to Diana, and which was built in the 2nd century. Opposite the columns of this temple is the former **Convent of Os Lóios**, now a *pousada nacional*, and the Church of **São João Baptista**, an excellent exponent of Manueline Gothic architecture.

The **Cathedral**, or **Sé**, whose origins go back to the 12th and 13th centuries, is an example of early Gothic architecture. Two imposing towers flank the portal, which features figures representing the twelve apostles. The most interesting elements in the cathedral interior are the high chapel, with its baroque altarpiece, the 16th-century oak organ and the various collections making up the Cathedral Treasure. The most outstanding exhibit in this treasure is a carving representing the Virgin of Paradise.

The **Church of São Francisco**, without doubt one of the most beautiful religious buildings in Évora, houses

THE BAROQUE STYLE IS ALSO PRESENT IN ÉVORA CATHEDRAL.

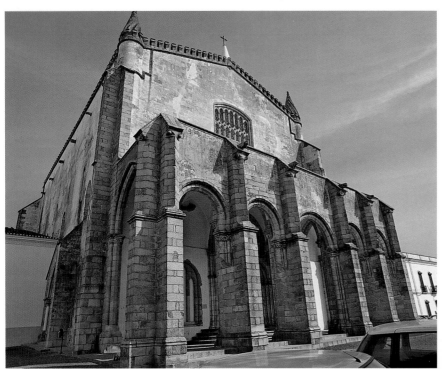

THE CHURCH OF SÃO FRANCISCO.

the curious "Chapel of Bones". In it, the tibiae, femura and skulls of the monks who lived here are used to cover the columns and arches, forming a surprising and macabre spectacle. Besides the city walls, other places of interest include the **churches of O Espíritu Santo and of Graça**, which reflect the influence of Italian Mannerism, the **City Museum**, with important artefacts from Roman times as well as a collection of Portuguese paintings, and the **Royal Palace of D. Manuel**, in one of whose rooms the great navigator and discoverer Vasco de Gama was made an admiral of the fleet.

PRAÇA DO GIRALDO, NERVE-CENTRE OF ÉVORA.

WITH 3,000 SUNSHINE HOURS PER YEAR, THE ALGARVE IS A VERITABLE TOURIST PARADISE. IN THE PHOTOGRAPH, CAPE SÃO VICENTE.

The Algarve looks out on the Atlantic from an infinity of lovely beaches which have made this one of the country's leading tourist destinations. With over 3,000 hours of sunshine per year, this southern region of Portugal has undergone a remarkable process of development in recent years, though it has wisely conserved all its many natural and scenic attractions.

The capital of the Algarve is **Faro**, a city which has grown accustomed to the bustle of thousands of visitors, to whom it offers a number of architectural and artistic jewels of outstanding interest. In the northern part of the city is the baroque Church of O Carmo, dating from the 18th century. The interior of this church is lavishly decorated with gilded carvings of the most exquisite taste. Also worth a visit are the Ethnographic Museum, with, amongst other exhibits, a series of models illustrating how the special tuna fishing nets are used; the Maritime Museum; the Church of São Pedro and the Church of A Mesicórdia, both with Renaissance portals.

Nevertheless, the main point of interest in Faro is the old city, crossing under the Arch of A Vila, in Praça Francisco Gomes, we enter a network of narrow streets whose air of distinction makes strolling around them an extraordinary pleasure. One of the main monuments in this part of the city is the cathedral, reformed on many occasions, though its original ground plan shows it to be a late-Romanesque con-struction. In the same square is the Episcopal Palace, its front richly adorned with glazed tiles. Still in this part of Faro, the City Archaeological Museum displays remains from the nearby Roman ruins of Estói. Particularly interesting is the mosaic devoted to Neptune and the four winds.

The town of **Estói** lies around twelve kilometres inland from Faro. Besides the lovely little Palace of the Viscount of Estói, a replica on a smaller scale of the Palace of Queluz, Estói attracts tourists in their thousands every year to visit the Roman ruins of Milréu. This settlement, known from the 2nd to the 6th centuries as Ossonoba, is considered the embryo of what later became the city of Faro. Remains of mosaics, thermal baths and

FARO: THE CHURCH OF O CARMO, THE CATHEDRAL AND THE PORT.

ROMAN MOSAIC IN ESTÓI.

columns are proof of the existence here of a Roman villa, though fragments of a Christian church have also been discovered. The period in which this was built makes it one of the oldest in the world.

East of Faro are the cities of **Olhão**, with the isles of Armona and Culatra, boasting paradisiacal beaches of the finest sand, **Tavira**, with its medieval air and Roman origins where we also find a tiny island of enormous dunes, and **Vila Real de Santo António** which, standing on the banks of the River Gua-

ROCHA BEACH IN PORTIMÃO.

OVERALL VIEW OF SILVES, FORMER CAPITAL OF THE ALGARVE.

diana, marks the frontier with Spain.

To the west, we come to town after town, their magnificent long beaches lined with hotels to accommodate the ever-increasing number of visitors to these parts. **Quarteira, Vilamoura, Albufeira, Porches,** famous for its ceramics, and **Lagos**, well-known for its wines, are just some of these fast-growing resorts.

OVERALL VIEW OF A PONTA DA PIEDADE, NEAR LAGOS.

OVERALL VIEW OF FUNCHAL.

The Archipelago of Madeira, made up of the islands of **Madeira, Porto Santo, Desertas** and **Selvagens**, lies some 975 kilometres from the south coast of Portugal and 545 kilometres as the crow flies from the African continent. Though different theories exist as to the origins and age of these islands, the most widely accepted is that the archipelago was formed by underwater volcanic eruptions some 25 or 30 million years ago. As for the discovery of Madeira, though earlier reference would appear to exist, history attributes this to the Portuguese navigator Juan Gonçales Zarco who came across them in 1419 after being blown off his course to Africa. Madeira has formed part of Portugal ever since, though with parentheses during which the islands were ruled by Spain (1580-1640) or England (during the Napoleonic wars).

Though the Desertas (desert) and Selvagens (savage) islands are uninhabited, Madeira and Porto Santo offer the visitor the most comfortable residential facilities and the warmest of welcomes. Nevertheless, and though the two are only 50 kilo-metres apart and both share a mountainous terrain, the landscape found on the two islands is completely different. Madeira has abundant water and trees, whilst Porto Santo is much more arid.

The island of Madeira, whose capital is **Funchal**, is 58 kilometres in length and 23 kilometres in width. A mountain chain of volcanic peaks, the highest reaching 1,861 metres, crosses the island from east to west. The mountainous terrain seems to loom over the sea, forming spectacular cliffs of the most astounding beauty.

MADEIRA IS PARTICULARLY RICH IN FLORA. IN THE PHOTOGRAPHS, FIVE VARIETIES OF ORCHID.

VIEW OF THE MOUNTAINS FROM O PICO DO AREEIRO.

RIBEIRA BRAVA CLIFFS.

Two views of Santana.

The port of Moniz.

ISLE OF SÃO MIGUEL: "LAKE OF THE SEVEN CITIES".

São Miguel, Santa Maria, Terceira, Graciosa, São Jorge, Pico, Faial, Flores and **Corvo** are the names of the nine islands of volcanic origin forming the Archipelago of the Azores, which lies some 1,400 kilometres from Europe and 3,900 kilometres from North America. Though the experts differ as to the date these mid-Atlantic islands were discovered, most historians attribute this to the Portuguese navigator Diego de Silves in 1427. There is more general agreement that the first colonists had settled here by the year 1432.

The archipelago gives its name to the Azores anticyclone, a centre of high pressure which generally ensures many hours of sunshine. Nevertheless, heavy rainfall can also occur here in just a short period of time, and generally with little notice. All these conditions have led to the existence of sub-tropical vegetation here which further enhances the natural beauty of these islands.

The largest of the Azores is the **Isle of São Miguel**, with its mountainous profile. Its principal town is **Ponta Delgada**, capital of the archipelago which, like that of Madeira, has been an autonomous region since 1976. On **Santa Maria**, further east, are several imposing fortresses, whilst other places of interest in the Azores include the city of **Angra do Heroísmo**, on **Terceira**, listed as World Cultural Heritage by UNESCO; the Caldeira volcano, on Graciosa; the splendid landscapes of Pico; the Isle of Faial, an immense volcanic mountain; the tiny villages on the cliffs of São Jorge; the lagoons of Flores; and the picturesque Isle of Corvo.

FURNAS (ISLE OF SÃO MIGUEL).

PONTA DELGADA (ISLE OF SÃO MIGUEL).

CONTENTS

EDITORIAL FISA ESCUDO DE ORO, S.A.
Tel: 93 230 86 00
www.eoro.com

I.S.B.N. 978-84-378-2187-0
Printed in Spain
Legal Dep. B. 11095-2011